SELENA GOMEZ
NATURAL STAR

SELENA GOMEZ
NATURAL STAR

By Riley Brooks

SCHOLASTIC INC.

New York Toronto London Auckland
Sydney Mexico City New Delhi Hong Kong

Flowers:
©BLUE67DESIGN/SHUTTERSTOCK
SELENA:
©GREGG DeGUIRE/PICTUREGROUP/APIMAGES
BACK COVER:
©Darren Calabrese/Associated Press

ISBN 978-0-545-42954-2

12 11 10 9 8 7 6 5 4 3 2 1   12 13 14 15 16/0
Printed in the U.S.A.   40

First printing, January 2012

CONTENTS

INTRODUCTION

When Selena Gomez arrived at the 2011 *Vanity Fair* party after the Academy Awards, she caught the attention of every photographer on the red carpet. Wearing an elegant red Dolce & Gabbana gown with picture-perfect makeup, Selena wowed the whole crowd. She'd definitely come a long way since she got her start on a kids' TV show in a small town in Texas. Her date for the evening, pop star Justin Bieber, posed next to her in a black suit with a red pocket square that matched her dress perfectly. The pair hadn't attended the awards show, but they were both excited to see their friends and peers at the after-party and mingle with directors and producers.

"It was like a little prom night, wasn't it?" Selena told David Letterman on his talk show. It was like prom for the two teen stars — well, a working prom! Selena was about to wrap up filming the final season of her hit Disney Channel show *Wizards of Waverly Place*, and was feeling a lot like most teens feel when they go to prom and graduate from high school. As much as Selena was sad to let go of her past, she was also feeling very excited and hopeful about her future, and ready to take her career to the next level with starring roles in some big movies.

As special as that night was, it was just the start of a year filled with big steps for Selena — from a third album and cross-country tour to a hit summer movie, Selena is making her mark in Hollywood in a big way. Selena's star is still on the rise, and there is really no limit to just how far she'll go!

CHAPTER 1:
Texas Sweetheart

It was a perfect summer day when Mandy and Ricardo Gomez welcomed their beautiful baby girl, Selena Marie Gomez, into the world on July 22, 1992. She was born in Grand Prairie, Texas. Her young parents were so thrilled with their newborn that they wanted to give her a name that she could carry proudly. They named her Selena Marie Gomez, after one of their favorite Mexican singers, superstar Selena Quintanilla-Pérez.

Ricardo Gomez, Selena's father, was originally from Guadalajara, Mexico. Selena's mother, Amanda, "Mandy," Cornett Gomez was born and raised in

Texas. The young parents had their hands full with their little one. Luckily they had a lot of support from their families.

When Selena was five years old, her parents made the tough decision to get a divorce. "There were a lot of tears," Selena confessed to M magazine. The divorce was hard for Selena, but she has remained close to both of her parents. And she knows that it was the right decision for both her mom and dad. Eventually Mandy married Brian Teefey from Michigan. Selena gets along well with her stepfather and she was very excited to see her mother so happy. ". . . I have a stepdad. And, honestly, I love him with all my heart. I see how happy my mom is with him, which is awesome," Selena told M magazine.

Selena loved growing up in Texas. She had both sides of the family nearby so she was never without plenty of love and support. "I've had the same friends since kindergarten, so everyone is still really close. And

I'm really close to all my family — my cousins, my aunts, my grandmother and grandpa," Selena told *Girls' Life* magazine.

As she got older, Selena grew into an adorable tomboy who was always playing outside. "We live in the nice suburb areas, and everybody knows everybody in that little neighborhood. We could all walk outside and hang out . . . You can go to skate parks, or you can go to the mall or movies with your friends," Selena explained to *Girls' Life* magazine.

Her guy friends may not have been into girly things, but they did teach Selena a lot about sports, and basketball is her favorite. She began playing when she was young, and even played on her school team for a while. "I used to be on a team for school, and then I got home-schooled, so not anymore . . . I'm a huge basketball fan. My favorite is the San Antonio Spurs . . . Back home, all my guy friends were Dallas Mavericks fans so it was kind of a competition between us, but usually my team would win," Selena joked to *Girls' Life* magazine.

When Selena wasn't outside with her friends, she was usually making art, reading, or watching movies! Selena loved getting a chance to express herself creatively, as she explained to *Scholastic News*: "I like to draw and paint. I've been doing it ever since I could remember. I have no idea what I draw. I just draw anything that comes to mind . . . I loved Dorothy and I loved the characters and I have the movie. I have no idea why, but I just loved that book [*The Wizard of Oz*]."

Selena is still very close with her friends and family in Grand Prairie. Selena goes home to visit as often as she can. "My mom has always told me, 'Remember where you came from.' I was surrounded by the best people back home. I'll never forget that," Selena told Discoverygirls.com.

With the support of her friends and family, Selena discovered a passion for performing that set her apart from the other kids her age. Mandy performed as a stage actress in local theater productions, and Selena loved watching her. She taught Selena that hard work and dedication really do pay off and that you always have to believe in yourself. Mandy even named her production company July Moon Productions after her biggest dream come true — Selena! "July" comes from the month that Selena was born, and Selena means "moon" in Greek.

With so much talent in her family, it's really no surprise that Selena set her sights on performing when she was just a little girl. ". . . I watched my mom do a lot of theater when I was younger and I saw how much passion she had for it. I loved to watch her rehearse. I always wanted to get involved in that," Selena shared with *Scholastic News*. When Selena was about six years old, she decided that she, too, wanted to be an actress. Selena's mom knew she needed to support her daughter's dreams, so she took Selena to her first audition. "I grew up around it [theater], and I just always loved it. I loved running lines with her, and then one day I tried out for something and got it, and it all started!" Selena told PBSKids.org.

Selena was a natural entertainer. She just seemed to know when to ham it up and when to tone it down. Selena always impressed casting agents with her comedic timing, but she was a little self-conscious about her looks. "I wanted to be like my friends, I hung out with girls who had blue eyes and blonde hair and I thought, 'I want to look like them!'" Selena explained to *TWIST* magazine. But Selena's more exotic look actually helped her when she began acting. And now she couldn't be more proud of her heritage. "When I went to auditions, I'd be in a room with a lot of blonde girls, and I always stood out. It actually helped . . . that I looked different. It got me where I am today! I don't know if I would have had the opportunity to be on *Wizards of Waverly Place* if it weren't for my heritage. I realize everybody wants what they don't have. But at the end of the day, what you have inside is much more beautiful than what's on the outside!" Selena told *TWIST* magazine.

By the time Selena was seven years old, she never could have imagined what was in store for her. Her birthday that year would change Selena's life more than she could ever have expected.

CHAPTER 2:
Bopping with Barney

Selena went to her very first audition in July, right around the time of her seventh birthday. "I got into it when I was six or seven. My mom did a lot of theater back in Dallas, Texas. I asked her if I could try acting, too. *Barney & Friends* was the first audition I went to and the first show I was ever on," Selena told *Time for Kids*.

The show Selena was auditioning for was the Public Broadcasting Service television series, *Barney & Friends*. It has been a huge hit with both kids and parents since 1992. It stars Barney, Baby Bop, BJ, and Riff, a group of loveable and colorful plush dinosaurs. They sing, dance, tell stories, and play games with a cast of talented elementary school kids.

Acting in the show was one of the best opportunities for kids in Texas to break into show business. That's why on one hot July morning, a long line of kids and their parents wound around the parking lot of The Studios at Las Colinas, Texas. The children waiting in line were there for an open audition and a chance to be series regulars on *Barney & Friends*. Most of them had no acting experience and ranged in age from five to ten years old, were of different races, and had dramatically different looks. Selena and her mom knew that the competition would be stiff, but they were willing to wait anyway, just for a shot at impressing the casting agents.

Selena was a little scared when it was her turn to audition. "I was definitely nervous; I was very shy when I was younger. . . . But then when I got to the audition, I realized it was just running lines, just like I always did with my mom. It was scary — and those situations are still scary for me — but it was fun at the same time," Selena told PBSKids.org. Even though she was nervous, Selena did a great job. She was called back to do a few more auditions, and then she got the call that she was on the show. She was so excited! Selena was cast as Gianna, and she was a hit from day one. She was funny and spunky, and a real asset to the show. In fact, Selena was often selected for funny scenes that required great comedic timing.

Acting on the show was a wonderful experience for Selena, and she believes that starring on *Barney & Friends* helped her become the professional actress she is today. Selena told the *OC Register*, "I actually learned a lot from [*Barney & Friends*], because I didn't know anything. That was my first audition, my first anything I'd ever done. I think that was a real blessing." Working on *Barney* taught Selena many basic acting skills. She learned how to memorize and deliver lines, how to work with other actors, how to sing and dance on camera, and how to work with multiple cameras. Selena told *Time for Kids*: "I was very shy when I was little. . . . I didn't know what 'camera right' was. I didn't know what blocking was. I learned everything from *Barney*."

Selena loved her work, and continued filming her role as Gianna on *Barney & Friends* for two seasons. She credits *Barney* not only with giving her a start in show business, but with helping her develop a real love for acting. ". . . A lot of people would be embarrassed to say they were on *Barney*, but I embrace the fact and I had such a wonderful time doing that show," Selena explained to Maggie Rodriguez on *The Early Show*.

Even though Selena's life as an actress was very cool, it wasn't always easy. Not everyone at Selena's school was supportive. In fact, some of Selena's so-called friends were very jealous of her success. "I'd miss a couple of weeks for *Barney* and then I'd go back to school and I'd deal with some jealousy. I wouldn't talk about the show unless somebody said, 'How was your episode?' So not a lot of people were jealous — just this one group of girls who didn't like me," Selena told DiscoveryGirls.com.

It was hard for Selena to deal with her friends turning on her like that. The girls were popular and they tried to make Selena look bad in front of all of their classmates. "Popularity isn't what you think it is," Selena tells *J-14* magazine. "It's much better to be yourself than trying to be cool. Popularity never leads to anything good." Rather than give in to the spiteful girls, Selena decided that they just weren't worth it. "You can't get involved, fire back, or do anything," Selena continued to *J-14* magazine "If people say, 'I heard you did this,' just say, 'I'm sorry, that's not true!' At the end of the day, I really ended up finding out who my true friends were."

Luckily, Selena had enough self-confidence to rise above the drama. She separated herself from them as much as she could and focused on her own things — and it definitely paid off in the long run! She hung out with her real friends and continued to focus on her career. "I mean, I got made fun of because I was in *Barney*! Just know that, at the end of the day, you will be okay and you'll always have your true friends with you," Selena said to DiscoveryGirls.com ". . . they've even come out to Los Angeles to see the show . . . I did lose a couple of friends because of the whole jealousy thing. But I look at it like a sport. Some kids play soccer. Acting is my sport."

Selena filmed episodes of *Barney & Friends* through the end of fifth grade. It was an amazing opportunity for Selena, and she wouldn't trade her time on the show for anything. There are very few people who can actually say that they got their show business start singing along with a large purple dinosaur named Barney!

CHAPTER 3:
The Road to Fame

After filming *Barney & Friends*, Selena knew that she wanted to be a professional actress for the long haul. To prepare for auditions, Selena took classes from Cathryn Sullivan at EveryBody Fits studio in Coppell, Texas. With Cathryn's help and encouragement, Selena's singing, acting, and dancing skills improved even more, and she began auditioning for new roles. Working with a coach made a big difference, but no one was harder on the budding star than herself. Selena took every bit of advice to heart and worked to make sure every monologue, song, and dance she performed was perfect.

Selena started out with auditions in Texas. With its generally pleasant weather and varied landscapes, Texas is a great place to shoot commercials, movies, and television shows. That was good news for Selena since it meant there were always auditions for her to go to. She landed parts in a number of commercials, and filmed national spots for Wal-Mart, Hasbro, and TGIFridays.

Then, when Selena was eleven years old, she landed her first cameo role in a major movie. It was a very small part of the "water park girl" in 2003's *Spy Kids 3-D: Game Over*, the third installment in Robert Rodriguez's *Spy Kids* movie franchise. Even though Selena's part was very small, it was a role in a feature film and Selena learned a lot and was so proud. Plus, going to the movies with friends to see herself in 3-D was totally cool! And the rest of the cast was incredible. Selena got to work with big-name stars like Alexa Vega, Daryl Sabara, Sylvester Stallone, Antonio

Banderas, and Salma Hayek. Working with Latina actress Salma especially inspired her, since Salma encouraged Selena to be proud of her own Mexican heritage.

Selena's next role was in a made-for-television movie of the popular show *Walker, Texas Ranger*. The film first aired on October 16, 2005. It was called *Walker, Texas Ranger: Trial by Fire* and Selena played the part of Julie. The show is about Cordell Walker, a Texas Ranger who takes the law into his own hands when dealing with criminals. The movie was a hit with *Walker* fans, and Selena enjoyed being a part of such a successful and long-running show about Texas. It was extra cool for her since she had watched it with her grandmother while she was growing up!

The next project that Selena landed was a pilot for a new children's show called *Brain Zapped*. Selena was cast in the lead role of Emily Garcia and she also recorded the show's theme song. The show was about reading and the adventures that can be found inside books. Most of the episode was shot on a green screen, which was a cool new experience for Selena. It meant that she did all her acting while standing in a special all-green room. Then, during the editing process, the editor replaces all the green with any pre-shot background for the scene. The green screen made it easy for the director to add special effects and to make it *seem* like Selena had journeyed back to prehistoric times with dinosaurs or to the North Pole. But in reality, Selena never had to leave Texas at all!

Unfortunately, a network never picked up *Brain Zapped*, which was a little disappointing for Selena. Luckily for Selena's fans, the pilot is available on DVD for anyone who wants to see it!

After *Brain Zapped* didn't pan out, Selena began to feel that she may have outgrown all of the acting opportunities in Texas, so when she heard about an open casting call in Dallas for the Disney Channel, she begged her mother to let her go. Little did Selena know that that audition would eventually make her a superstar!

CHAPTER 4:
Disney Dreams

In the summer of 2006, the Disney Channel began a casting search for promising young talent. Selena attended the local audition in nearby Dallas, Texas, with her mom. Selena was only twelve years old, but she knew it was the chance of a lifetime! Wearing an adorable blue poncho, Selena was definitely nervous, knowing that she would be competing against thousands of other talented girls, but she was ready for the challenge. She was charming, spunky, and made the casting directors take serious notice.

In fact, the folks at Disney were so impressed with her tape that three weeks later they asked Selena to audition again with a very select group of candidates for the head honchos at Disney. "They flew us out to California. It was definitely scary. I was in this room full of executives and I was testing against girls who have done movies," Selena explained to *Variety*. Even though Selena was facing some pretty intense competition, she aced the audition.

One of the executives supervising Selena's audition was Gary Marsh, the president of entertainment for Disney Channel Worldwide. Gary told *Entertainment Weekly* that Selena's audition was "green, it was rough — but she had that 'It Factor.'" Since Gary was in charge of casting and developing new series for the Disney Channel, he was an expert at recognizing rising talent when he saw it! "We don't look at television as the endgame," he explained to *Entertainment Weekly*. "That's the launch pad . . . We go into this thinking we are going to build a star; it's not thinking we are casting a role." Gary and the rest of the Disney executives definitely wanted Selena Gomez to become part of the Disney family. That was music to Selena's ears and she happily agreed to get to work!

First, Disney asked Selena to film the pilot for *What's Stevie Thinking?* a spin-off of the hit Disney series *Lizzie McGuire*. Selena had so much fun shooting the pilot and working with the cast and crew. They were all very proud of *What's Stevie Thinking?* but unfortunately test audiences weren't as interested in the show as the Disney Channel had hoped they would be. A year after filming, Selena got the news that Disney decided not to pick up the series. She was pretty disappointed, but hoped that her chance would come soon.

Even though *What's Stevie Thinking?* didn't make it into production, filming the pilot had generated a lot of exposure for Selena in Hollywood. Soon, Disney's biggest competitor, Nickelodeon, contacted Selena. Selena and her agent met several times with their development executives and she even auditioned for a Nickelodeon pilot and a made-for-television movie. But somehow Nickelodeon just didn't click for Selena. "It was uncomfortable," she explained to *Entertainment Weekly*, "like I was cheating on Disney." Selena felt completely comfortable and at home with the Disney Channel, and really wanted to work there. It was obvious that Disney wanted to keep Selena, too! They weren't willing to let her go to their rival network. For the next television season, Gary was developing two new pilots and he offered starring roles in both to Selena. It was an exciting time, since Selena knew at least one of the pilots would get picked up and make it on the air.

A spin-off of *The Suite Life of Zack and Cody* was the first new pilot. The show starred Arwin, the maintenance man from the Tipton Hotel. In the show, he moves in with his sister to help her look after her kids. Selena was cast as one of Arwin's nieces, Chloe. Ultimately, the show didn't test well with audiences and Disney decided to move on to the next pilot for Selena instead.

The second pilot, called *Wizards of Waverly Place* was a comedy about a family of wizards living in New York City. The three siblings, Justin, Alex, and Jake, were secretly learning to use their magic, while going to school and helping their parents run a sandwich shop. The show was a unique mix of comedy and special effects that was perfect for Selena. Selena plays Alex, the only girl in the family, and the most mischievous and challenging character on the show. The test audiences absolutely loved it! Disney signed Selena up for the first season and then locked the rest of the cast in place.

Selena was super excited about the show, but she was less excited about moving to Los Angeles full-time. "The biggest challenge was moving away from home, and at first, I didn't know how I was gonna do it. Once I came out to L.A. and started working, I adjusted a little bit but I'm still a Texas girl," Selena explained to *Popstar!* Since Disney needed Selena in Hollywood as soon as possible, she and her mom moved to Los Angeles right away. Selena knew she was very lucky to have such a supportive family that was willing to help her achieve her dreams, no matter what it took! "It was sad to say good-bye to my friends and family, but it was a happy moment, too. They were so proud of me for achieving my dreams," Selena told Discoverygirls.com.

As soon as she moved, Disney was ready to put Selena to work. They booked her in guest appearances and promotional spots so that Disney fans could get to know Selena before her show aired.

Selena was a guest star on two of Disney's most popular shows at the time, *Hannah Montana* and *The Suite Life of Zack and Cody*. Selena's first guest role was on *The Suite Life of Zack and Cody*, in an episode called "A Midsummer's Nightmare." Selena played Gwen, the character who was dating Cody. During the episode, all the kids tried out for a production of *A Midsummer Night's Dream*. When Selena's character had to kiss Dylan Sprouse's character in the play, crazy

Selena with Justin Bieber on the red carpet.

Selena and her mom at a **charity event.**

SELENA
performing at the 2011
Teen Choice Awards.

Selena posing with her costars at the *Monte Carlo* premiere.

SELENA and Joey King at the premiere of *Ramona and Beezus.*

SELENA accepting the 2011 Nickelodeon Kids' Choice Award for "Favorite TV Actress."

© ASSOCIATED PRESS

© ASSOCIATED PRESS

Selena and her **best friend** Taylor Swift.

Selena and the cast of *Wizards of Waverly Place* celebrate their **Emmy win** for "Outstanding Children's Program."

things began to happen! Gwen liked kissing Zack so much that she dumped Cody. Then the brothers got into a huge and very goofy fight onstage during the play.

It was a fun episode to film and it was also a big first for Selena as an actress and as a teenager — she got her very first kiss! ". . . my first was with Dylan on *The Suite Life of Zack and Cody*. That was fun. He was shorter than me, so I had to bend down a little bit, but it was a cute episode," Selena told *Girls' Life* magazine. Selena handled it really well, even though she was probably pretty nervous about having her very first kiss in front of all the cast and crew and her mom! Luckily, both twins were super nice and they've stayed good friends with Selena.

Next, Selena was invited to guest star on *Hannah Montana*. She played Hannah's biggest rival, Mikayla, who was an up and coming pop diva bent on stealing all of Hannah's fans. Selena had a blast playing mean girl Mikayla. Fans loved her so much that Selena was asked to appear as Mikayla on several more episodes. It was really a fun part to play, battling Hannah for awards, fans, and cute guys!

With several popular guest spots to her credit, Selena was more than ready to begin filming her own show. Once she walked onto the set of the *Wizards of Waverly Place* and the cameras started rolling, she blew everyone away with her spunk, talent, and comedic timing. The Disney Channel knew right away that they had a hit on their hands. Selena Gomez had finally made it — and Disney would never be the same!

CHAPTER 5:
Wizards of Waverly Place

In 2007, Selena's dream to star in a Disney Channel original series finally came true. She started filming the first season of *Wizards of Waverly Place*.

Wizards of Waverly Place is all about the Russo family. The Russos own and run a neighborhood sandwich shop on Waverly Place in New York City called the Waverly Sub Station. To the public the Russos seem like the average New York family, but they actually have a very big secret — each of the three Russo kids has magical powers!

Justin, played by David Henrie, Alex, played by Selena, and Max, played by Jake T. Austin, have inherited magical powers from their dad, Jerry. Unfortunately, only one child from each wizard family is allowed to keep his or her magical powers as an adult. After they come of age, a family competition will determine who gets to keep their wizard status. Until then, all three kids must learn as much as they can about using their magic. "The kids are learning magic from their father. But at the same time, we still go to school and deal with issues that any other normal teenager would. Our friends and classmates don't know that we can do magic, so we lead kind of a double life," Selena explained to *Time for Kids*. Of course, having magical powers sounds really cool, but they also get the Russos into a lot of very funny situations.

Family is a big part of *Wizards*, since the whole Russo family definitely has to work together to keep their magic a secret from the rest of the world. When Dad, Jerry Russo, played by David DeLuise, isn't running the sandwich shop, he is holding daily wizard training classes in their home's secret "lair." Jerry lost his own magical abilities when his brother became the family wizard, but he is a great teacher. Alex and Max aren't always the best students, but Jerry does his best to teach the kids the proper way to perform spells and use magical objects. His most difficult challenge is helping clean up his kids' magical messes when they don't follow his rules!

Of course, Jerry does have help from his wife, Theresa Russo, played by Maria Canals Berrera. While helping to run the sandwich shop, she teaches her children the importance of their Latino heritage, offers motherly advice, and tries to stay one step ahead of her children's mishaps, magical or otherwise. "It is a lot of fun to be the Disney mom. [It] is what I feel like I am. Especially because the parts have been so well written, so beautifully written, the parents have been so integral to the story. . . . I love playing Theresa!" Maria told *TV Guide*. Theresa is Mexican and Jerry's family is Italian, so they try to integrate traditions from both sides of the family into their kids' lives.

Justin is the oldest Russo child. He is disciplined, studious, and a total overachiever. He desperately wants to be cool, and his siblings tease him a lot for being a nerd. But when Alex and Max get into trouble, Justin is always there to help them out of it. "He [Justin] tends to do what is right, and he keeps everyone in check," David Henrie told *TV Guide*.

Unlike her big brother, Alex is not disciplined, studious, or much of an overachiever. Instead, Alex loves to have a good time and will go out of her way to avoid hard work, but she has a good heart and always does the right thing in the end. "Alex is the only girl of the three kids, so she has their dad wrapped around her finger. Also, because she's been raised with boys her entire life, she's got a little tomboyish twist. Alex is the sibling who gets into the most trouble," Selena explained to *Time for Kids*. Alex is spunky and popular and never hesitates to use her magic to take the easy way out. In fact, "'cast magic first, ask questions later' is her motto," according to Disney.com.

The youngest Russo sibling, Max, has just come into his powers, so he is not quite as far along in his magical training as Justin and Alex. But what Max lacks in magic, he makes up for in comedy! Max isn't particularly smart and his whacky, zany, and somewhat dimwitted ideas are always hilarious. Max and Alex get along very well on the show and often team up to pull a prank on Justin.

Of course, it isn't all in the family! Alex's best friend is Harper, played by Jennifer Stone. Harper is a wannabe fashionista who loves wearing wacky themed outfits — like a dress covered in rubber duckies or an entire outfit made of waxed fruit! Harper eventually finds out that Alex is a wizard and even moves in with the Russo family when her parents have to go out of the country. Since Alex is always in trouble, Harper is often her partner in crime. Harper also spends a lot of time trying to get Justin to notice her since she has a huge crush on him!

Alex, Justin, and Max also had various friends, boyfriends, and girlfriends played by some awesome guest stars — like *Good Luck Charlie*'s Bridgit Mendler, *Pretty Little Liars*' Lucy Hale, and *Hannah Montana*'s Moisés Arias. Working with new guest stars was always a blast for the whole cast — and who wouldn't want to join in on the *Wizards*' magic?

Selena loves playing Alex, but it hasn't always been easy to get into character. Selena is sweet, hardworking, and very responsible, so playing sassy, troublemaker Alex has been a challenge! But it was really fun for Selena to step outside of her comfort zone and bring such a cool character to life. Luckily, the writers and producers of the show trusted Selena's instincts and really let Selena give Alex her own twists. "I asked that they keep her edgy, I don't want to be wearing heels. She wears Converse, and she's cool. I'm not really a girly girl," Selena told *Entertainment Weekly* at the start of season one.

As the series has progressed Alex has become more and more of a troublemaker, but that's okay with Selena. As she explained to *Teen* magazine, that's one of Selena's favorite parts about playing Alex, ". . . she's always getting into trouble and she's doing stuff that I wish I could do. At the end of the day it's all fake! I don't want to get in trouble and make a mess, but it's nice to pretend that it was real!"

In some of Selena's favorite episodes, Alex finds herself in very big trouble! As she told PBSKids.org, "The *quinceañera* episode was probably my favorite, or the episode where Alex wanted to go to a rated R movie. She tries to put a spell on herself to magically go into the movie theater, but she ends up actually *in* the movie, so she's stuck in this scary movie sorority-house flick, and they shot it just like a movie. It was so much fun because it was like being able to shoot an actual scary movie." Getting to be the troublemaker is always fun for Selena. She'd never break the rules or talk back to her parents in real life, but getting to do it on the show is pretty cool. That way she gets to have the fun — but she never gets grounded.

Selena and her *Wizards of Waverly Place* family have learned a lot about working with unusual sets and magical, special effects props. "It's pretty cool. We've been up in harnesses. We've worked with animals and voiceovers . . . The special effects add a different level to the Disney Channel," Selena told *Time for Kids*. In fact, the cast has done some pretty crazy things while filming *Wizards of Waverly Place*. "Oh, man! Where do I begin? I've had to pour chocolate all over myself. I've had mashed potatoes in my hair. We've 'flown' magic carpets. I get turned into [a] tiger in one episode! I think this show's all about the craziness, and we've done a lot of crazy stuff here," Selena explained to *Time for Kids.*

"The show is definitely different from other Disney Channel shows," Selena told *Time for Kids.* Whether it's learning to drive a magic carpet or conjuring up a pocket elf to help with a Spanish test, the Russo kids learn the good, the bad, and the often very funny consequences of using their magic. When asked by *Teen* magazine if she believed in magic, Selena said, "I think a little bit, I kind of do. I think it's cool to sort of step into something supernatural." Before taking on the role of Alex, Selena had never been much of a fan of fantasy, so she had to do her homework on all things wizard-related fast!

Magic is such a fun part of *Wizards of Waverly Place.* What kind of spell would Selena perform if she were a wizard? She told *Time for Kids,* "I've always wanted to be able to zap food to anywhere at any time. For example, if you're sitting on the couch craving pizza, you could say a spell, and boom! It's right there." What other magic from the show does she wish she could do in real life? "Clone myself! Just to get out of class, it would be nice!" Selena said laughingly to *Teen* magazine.

It must be a lot of fun to film the scenes with special effects, but Selena also enjoys the scenes that involve the entire Russo family. Selena told PBSKids.org, "My favorite scenes are ones where all of the family is together. Whether it's a funny or dramatic scene, whether we're trying to solve a problem or doing magic or turning my brother invisible, it comes off best when we're with the whole family in the loft. I think when we're all together the show is at its strongest point. And I love being with the entire cast in a scene."

Disney Channel executives were certainly right to believe that the show would be a success! After the premiere of *Wizards of Waverly Place* on October 12,

2007, they were thrilled as the popularity of the show grew with each episode that aired. It was such a hit that they filmed four seasons of the show before calling it quits. In addition to the regular episodes, the cast filmed a special Disney Channel original made-for-TV movie set in tropical Puerto Rico and multiple one-hour specials that feature supernatural creatures like werewolves, vampires, and even angels!

Fans definitely love the show, and they've proved it, voting the show for several awards. *Wizards of Waverly Place* has won multiple Nickelodeon Kid's Choice Awards, People's Teen Choice Awards, and even a Daytime Emmy! It meant so much to Selena that her peers and fans loved the show enough to vote for it during awards season.

But the best part of the show was how close Selena grew to her costars. Selena told *Teen* magazine, "It's been so much fun just to develop a new family and to have new friends. They're my second family, and everyone on there is so nice and so sweet. They're my real brothers and second parents!" Selena loves her television brothers, David and Jake, and considers them to be some of her best friends. Hanging out with them on the set all day is really fun for her. "I can't even explain it! I am very confident when I say that we are the closest cast that the Disney Channel has ever had. We've been told that because we spend every waking moment with each other — it's insane! Jake [Austin], Jen [Stone], David [Henrie], and I do karaoke together, we go to the movies, and we go surfing every weekend. And as soon as we get off work, we text and call each other. My mom is always like, 'You act like you never see each other!' We've just gotten so close," Selena told DiscoveryGirls.com.

When Jake, David, Jen and Selena aren't filming, they enjoy sitting around and talking between shoots, Selena explained to *Girls' Life* magazine. "Well, David has these cards with questions like, 'Would you treat your kids the way your parents treat you?' They're conversation cards, and you can ask each other what's your embarrassing moment and stuff. Other than that, we talk and laugh. If we're tired, we all just lounge together. David likes to hit the back of my knee so I almost trip. He's always doing that. We just get silly and play patty-cake or something." Selena texts and e-mails her friends from her trailer, gossips with Jen, and shoots hoops with Jake. "We actually have [a basketball court] on set. It's fun," Selena told *Girls' Life* magazine. "I only take on [my TV brother], so when I beat him it's not a good feeling. He's only twelve and half the time he beats me."

Jake also taught Selena how to surf, as she explained to PBSKids.org, "Yes, Jake recently did a movie where he surfed, and he told me I should try it. And I was like, 'Okay,' and I got really into it, it was so much fun. At first the ocean scared me a little bit, but we don't go too far out. Once you ride that first wave, there's something about it that keeps you riding more and more! . . . It's a stress relief. . . . It's nice to go on a beach and just forget about stuff and get away. It's fun. And acting's kind of like a sport for me, too, it's the same as something like football or basketball for other people. It's something you do for fun and something you're serious about." Now Selena is totally hooked and surfs as much as she can.

Spending so much time with David and Jake has been good for Selena. "I'm the only child, so it's really cool to play the middle sister of two brothers on *Wizards*. It's cool to pretend I've known these people all my life and get in fights with them. It's really fun," Selena tells *Girls' Life* magazine. It's the first time she has experienced what it would be like to have brothers, and she loves it! She further explains to PBSKids.org, "They basically ARE my brothers; they're my real family. My mom laughs at me all the time because we're constantly in touch with one another off the set, we're always calling. They're always there for me, and it's torture when I can't see them every day. We do fight like brothers and sisters sometimes, but mostly we play around and joke around. I don't have any siblings so this way I can have brothers." Selena even admitted to *Girls' Life* magazine, "I cried when the first season was over because my little brother [Jake T. Austin] was going back to New York, and my older brother [David Henrie] was going to Utah to shoot *Dadnapped*. So we call each other every day, 'What are you doing? I miss you.'"

So, what is the most surprising part about having "brothers"? Selena tells PBSKids.org, "They're both so protective of me. Even when I like a boy or something, they have to make sure he's okay, or the boy has to be 'approved' by them." Selena and Jennifer are good friends in real life, too. "Actually we [Selena and Jennifer] don't fight as much as Alex and Harper do. They have fights almost every episode — that's only because it's a part of growing up, but for us, we're just kinda chill. I think we're the opposite of Alex and Harper!" Selena tells *TV Guide*.

Of course, it's not all fun on the set. Selena, Jen, and Jake all spend the legally required limit of five hours a school day with a tutor on-set and their shooting schedule allows plenty of time for study! They have to finish their homework before they can do anything else. But when the stars aren't filming a scene or sitting in class, they can relax and hang out.

Fans easily relate to the Russo siblings on *Wizards of Waverly Place*, even though they don't have magic themselves because the characters are so realistic. After all, the show is really about family and everyone can relate to that. Episodes cover issues that everyone can relate to: sports, fashion, drama, school work, jobs, school, grades, crushes, dating, dances, friends, and family. "There are always times when you wish you could be invisible when something embarrassing happens. Or you wish you could rewind time because you just tripped in front of everybody. That's why I think kids will like the show. We bring to life everything that they imagine and dream about," Selena explained to *Time for Kids*.

The show came to an end after the fourth season. It was a bittersweet moment for Selena — while she didn't want to leave behind her friends in the cast, she knew that other exciting opportunities were just around the corner!

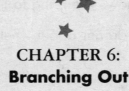

CHAPTER 6:
Branching Out

As much as Selena loved working on a TV show, she'd always dreamed of being in movies. She knows it's important for her career that she tries her hand at something new once in a while. During her summers off from *Wizards of Waverly Place*, Selena used the time to audition for new roles and film movies.

Selena is very particular about the types of roles she takes on. She doesn't say yes to just anything. She only accepts roles that she thinks will broaden her acting skills and appeal to her current fans. Selena reads every script her agent sends her very carefully and always talks them over with her parents. She also stays away from roles that she feels won't be challenging enough or roles that will limit her ability to book other roles in the future.

Selena actually turned down a starring role in both *High School Musical 3*, the first feature film in the Disney *High School Musical* franchise, and *Camp Rock* with the Jonas Brothers, for just that reason. Selena explained to the *New York Daily News*, "I passed on it because I didn't want to do it. I plan to take other roles in acting that are challenging for me." Selena has to take roles because they appeal to her, and it's really wonderful that she trusts her own judgment so much. It shows just how much confidence Selena has in herself and her abilities.

One role that really did appeal to Selena was providing the voice for Helga in the animated smash hit, *Horton Hears a Who!*, based on the classic Dr. Seuss story. "I had never done animation, so I thought it would be cool to try something different," Selena told the *New*

York Daily News. "I remember reading his books like crazy with my grandmother when I was younger," she added. Selena has long been a Dr. Seuss fan and she loved the story. *Horton Hears a Who!* is the story of an elephant named Horton who discovers an entire world of creatures called Whos existing on a daisy. Horton befriends one of the Whos, and decides it's up to him to keep them safe. Horton then must face some dangerous and often silly situations before he gets the Whos and their world to a safe place. The film builds upon the original book, expanding the characters and their world, and breathing new life into the familiar story.

Getting the opportunity to bring one of her favorite childhood books to life would be cool for anyone, but what made the film even cooler were Selena's amazing costars. Famous comedians played the two largest roles in the film. Horton was played by Jim Carrey and The Mayor of Whoville was played by Steve Carell. Selena played Steve Carell's daughters in the film — all ninety of them! They were all named Helga and since they each had a different look and personality, Selena had to come up with a different voice for each. "I voiced all of them," Selena explained to the *New York Daily News*. "I had to change up my voice to do higher voices, and then bring it down to do lower voices. All of the mayor's daughters look different so I play many different characters."

Selena was definitely excited to work alongside some of the biggest names in comedy, and she was ready to show them what she could do. Unfortunately, the complicated recording schedules meant that Selena never actually acted alongside her on-screen dad, Steve Carell. They recorded in completely separate sessions, not that anyone can tell from the finished movie — it sounds like they were in the same room! Selena was a little disappointed. She has really been looking forward to meeting Steve. "It was kind of a bummer! But at the same time, it was cool. I can see him and say 'Hey,

I played your daughter!" Selena told the *New York Daily News*. Hopefully, Selena will get the chance to act alongside Steve again—and this time actually come face-to-face with him!

The next role that Selena took on was much bigger. She landed the lead part of Mary in *Another Cinderella Story*. It was the straight-to-DVD follow-up film to 2004's *A Cinderella Story* starring Disney alum Hilary Duff and *One Tree Hill's* Chad Michael Murray. "It is not the sequel to the first one with Hilary Duff," Selena explained to the *New York Daily News*. "Instead, it's a take on the same basic premise — a modern version of the classic story of Cinderella. At a ball, I meet a guy and we fall in love during a dance. Instead of dropping my glass slipper, I drop my MP3 player." Mary, Selena's character, is a hip-hop and tango dancer and over the course of the story she got to do some amazing dance sequences with her love interest in the film, Joey Parker.

Andrew Seeley (Drew for short) played the part of Joey, and was best known as the singing voice for Zac Efron in Disney's *High School Musical*. He also co-wrote the Emmy-nominated song, "Get'cha Head in the Game" from the film. With Drew's great voice, natural charisma, and dance expertise, he was a natural fit for the role of Joey. Both Drew and Selena did some singing in the film, much to the delight of Selena's fans. Mary was a fun character and the singing and challenging dance routines were an incredible part of the movie. Hopefully Selena will get more chances to showcase her many talents in the future!

Selena had another Disney dream come true when she starred as Carter in the Disney Channel Original movie *Princess Protection Program* in June 2009. It was a huge hit with Disney fans and a lot of fun for Selena. They filmed in sunny Puerto Rico and Selena got to spend a lot of down time at the beach with her costars. It was more like a vacation than work!

In the movie, when Princess Rosalinda's country is threatened with invasion by an evil dictator, she is rescued by the Princess Protection Program, a top secret agency dedicated to the protection of princesses in peril. Rosalinda is sent to live with Mason, an agent in the program in Louisiana. Mason has a teenage daughter named Carter, who he expects to help him keep Princess Rosalinda safe. So Rosalinda becomes Rosie, an ordinary teenager, and goes to school with Carter. Carter isn't happy to have to babysit a princess, and the two girls don't get along at first. Carter is insecure and a total tomboy. She pretends like she doesn't care about being popular, but she secretly dreams of dating her crush, Donny, the cutest guy in town. Rosie fits right in at school and quickly becomes super popular, which only makes the two girls clash more. Eventually Carter teaches Rosie to be a normal teen and Rosie helps Carter learn to relax and be herself around the boy of her dreams. The two girls become close friends and learn a lot from each other. Selena brought her comedic timing to the set, earning lots of laughs from viewers. Plus, she showed true depth in some really touching moments.

Selena loved all of the projects she was working on, but she never stopped dreaming about starring in feature films. Luckily, she didn't have to wait long for those big dreams to come true!

CHAPTER 7:
Big Screen Dreams

Selena has been pursuing acting since she was six, so seeing her face up on the big screen has always been one of her biggest goals. She finally achieved it when she was cast as "Beezus" in *Ramona and Beezus*, the film adaptation of the beloved Beverly Cleary book *Beezus and Ramona*. The cast included adorable Joey King as Ramona and big name stars Ginnifer Goodwin, Bridget Moynahan, John Corbett, and Josh Duhamel. Selena's character, Beezus, is neat, studious, responsible, and above all, sensible, while her little sister Ramona is accident-prone, rambunctious, and always getting into trouble. Although Beezus is frequently annoyed with Ramona (and vice versa), she takes care of her little sister, defending and supporting her when needed.

With its star-studded cast, family-friendly message, and emotional characters, Selena knew working on *Beezus and Ramona* would help her grow and develop as an actress — and she knew her fans would love it, too! *Ramona and Beezus* premiered on July 23, 2010. Selena's fans loved it and it was a hit with families. Selena was really proud of her work, especially since her first starring role was in a family-friendly movie that all of her fans could enjoy!

Selena followed up with a starring role in June 2011's *Monte Carlo* alongside Katie Cassidy and Leighton Meester. A total chick flick, *Monte Carlo* is a fun film about three girls on the vacation of a life-time after graduating from high school. Selena plays "Grace," a sweet girl who is mistaken for a British heiress while on vacation, which leads to great adventures for her and her friends. It was a favorite in theaters with moms and daughters, and is the perfect DVD to rent for sleepovers! It was Selena's first headlining role in a film and there was a lot of pressure on her to give a perfect performance. Of course, Selena pulled it off in a big way — proving to every director and producer that she has real star power. With two fantastic films under her belt, she's sure to be starring in many more movies soon!

CHAPTER 8:
Making Music

Selena is always going to be an actress, but she has an incredible voice and enjoys music, too. As soon as she landed the role of Alex, Disney brought Selena into the studio to record the theme song for *Wizards of Waverly Place*. Selena had a blast recording "Everything Is Not What It Seems." It's a fun, upbeat pop song that gets stuck in fans' heads all the time. It was pretty cool for Selena to hear herself singing that song and know that it would open her show!

Next Selena went back into the studio to record a cover of a classic Disney song, "Cruella De Vil." The original song is from the 1961 Disney animated movie

101 Dalmatians, and it was the theme song of the movie's villainess, Cruella De Vil. Selena's version has a really modern twist and the music video she did for it was a hit with fans. It's very upbeat and totally fun to groove to!

"I think you can be more of yourself when you're singing. You can have a little bit more control over it. It's a different process, with going into the studio and not having to worry about what you look like on camera. You write music and perform it, have fun, then go in concert and jam out in front of an audience," Selena told PBSKids.org.

Selena was really getting excited about recording music, and the opportunities just kept on coming! Selena laid down tracks for several songs for *Another Cinderella Story* next. The pop music was fun, hip-hop infused, and perfect for dancing. She recorded "Tell Me Something I Don't Know" and "Bang a Drum." Selena and costar Drew Seeley also recorded the duet, "New

Classic," for the movie. Of course, Disney had other projects for her, too, so it wasn't long before Selena headed back to the Disney Studios to record "Fly to Your Heart," a new song for the animated *Disney Fairies* DVD *Tinker Bell.* Next, Selena and David Henrie recorded a song called "Make It Happen," which premiered in an episode of *Wizards of Waverly Place* in 2009!

Hollywood Records took notice of Selena's vocal talents and, in 2008, just before Selena's sixteenth birthday, she signed a record deal with Hollywood Records. Selena immediately went to work getting her band together and developing material to use for her debut album. "I would like all guys in the band," she laughed to *BOP* magazine. "I'm looking for someone who's very passionate about music and can show me that they can rock out. I like having people with me to lean on and write with and have fun with." Selena was super excited to develop her own sound and share her love of music with her fans. "I want to do music that is fun. I don't want to do anything where people are like, 'Oh wow, she's trying to get too deep and serious,' I want to do something that everyone will jam out to."

Selena has so many friends in the music business that she'd like to record and perform with. She shared with AceShowbiz.com that she'd love to work with Taylor Swift in the near future, adding that the girls have already chatted about it. "We have talked about a duet," Selena explained. "I think it would be really neat to have the country vibe."

Selena also recently worked with one of her favorite bands from Texas — Forever The Sickest Kids. She added vocals to one of their songs. They blogged about her visit on their official website: "We got a surprise visit today at the studio by a very special lady. Selena came by to hang — she is so super fun and one of the most talented, down-to-earth friends we have ever met

. . . we just had the most rockin' time ever with her and are pullin' super hard for her and her new album!" No matter who Selena works with, the result is always amazing!

Of course, Selena had very particular ideas about who she wanted to be as a singer. She told *MTV News*, "I'm not a solo artist. I will be singing, and I'm learning drums and playing electric guitar. I basically want to make music that is fun and that parents and kids can jump around to and have a good time to. Once I come out with my music, you're going to see a whole different side of me . . . different hair, different clothing, different attitude." Selena hopes her fans love her music as much as she does. "Most of my songs are about love," Selena told *J-14* magazine. "I am a sixteen-year-old teenager, and I sing about what is on every girl's mind — love!"

Selena Gomez and the Scene is the name of Selena's band. When their first album, *Kiss and Tell*, released on September 29, 2009, it quickly became a favorite with her fans, selling over 60,000 copies in the first week. A few months later, the band went on a yearlong tour to promote the album. Being on tour has been Selena's favorite part of her music career. She loves the rush of being on stage! The album's singles raced up the charts and fans couldn't get the catchy tunes out of their heads.

A year later, the band released their second album, *A Year Without Rain*, on September 21, 2010. They recorded all of the songs while on tour, and Selena was definitely inspired by life on the road. She wanted her sophomore album to be fun and perfect for parties. The final result was a series of dance-friendly tracks with electric beats.

Selena's third album, *When the Sun Goes Down*, hit store shelves on June 28, 2011, and it was the perfect summer album. Fans loved singing along to Selena's girl-power anthem "Who Says" at the beach and at pool parties. She toured all over the U.S. with her band to promote it, and sold out almost every show. If you haven't seen her live yet, don't worry — she's not done touring yet! So keep an eye out for Selena Gomez and the Scene at your local concert hall.

CHAPTER 9:
Hanging Out

Selena might be a big star these days, but when she's at home she's just a regular girl. Her mom, Mandy, and stepdad, Brian, expect Selena to help around the house and do chores just like her fans do! Mandy told *People*, "She has to do her own laundry. If she cooks, I clean. If I cook, she cleans. She has to help feed the dogs. There are really no set chores. We just all pitch in when needed . . . Selena knows who she is, and I am around to make sure she doesn't change."

Selena's parents are very serious about making sure she has the supervision and the support she needs. "My mom is my best friend. She's always with me everywhere I go. Sometimes on set, I just need to see her face. I'm like, 'Mom, I need to see you.' I just have to have my mom," Selena explained to *Girls' Life* magazine. Of course, Selena is growing up too. She's lucky that her parents know when to step in and help out and when to let Selena make her own decisions.

Selena doesn't get to see her dad and her extended family as much as she wants to because she is busy filming for various projects, traveling, or working in the recording studio. But she takes any chance she gets to go home to Texas. Selena gets pretty homesick when she goes too long between visits, as she revealed to *TigerBeat* magazine. "I think about home a lot. I don't get to go home to Texas often. I miss my family. They're the reason I am the person I am today." Selena's family is very understanding. With e-mail and lots of phone calls, they keep in touch pretty regularly when she can't make a trip home.

There are a few more important family members that

Selena always makes time for — her dogs! Selena has always loved animals and her dogs are a part of the family. "My family has four dogs — and there's a great trail by our house where we love to take them hiking!" Selena told Hollyscoop.com. Selena has even gotten involved with a charity in Puerto Rico to help homeless dogs and cats there. Selena filmed a "Dogumentary" about all of the stray animals out on the streets of Puerto Rico and has joined forces with Charity Buzz to benefit Island Dog, Inc. She has blogged about her new pet project and encouraged fans to donate money to the great charity.

When she's not hanging out with her family, Selena keeps busy with her close friends. She and her *Wizards* costars are very close. An only child, Selena says that David Henrie and Jake T. Austin "have become like my real brothers. By that I mean we fight and argue, too," she told the *OC Register*. "We do the whole, like, picking on each other brotherly-sister thing." Of course,

Selena has made some famous pals off of the show as well — like country superstar Taylor Swift and pop sensation Justin Bieber. Selena and Taylor have girly weekends away and can really relate when it comes to the pressures they both face in the spotlight. Selena and Justin Bieber have been spotted at events and even on vacation together. They always have a blast hanging out and seem to bring out the best in each other!

So what do Selena and her friends do when they get together? She loves to stay active, playing basketball and surfing. Selena told DiscoveryGirls.com, "My idea of getting away is going surfing. I've surfed six hours in one day!" Selena also loves going shopping and having sleepovers with her girlfriends. "I unwind by having movie nights with friends. I love nineties horror movies — they're more funny than scary," Selena told Hollyscoop.com. You won't find Selena snacking on popcorn or candy while watching her favorite flicks. Instead you might find her snacking on a nice, crunchy pickle. "I just love pickles, I guess I'm a sour girl," Selena told *Girls' Life* magazine. Where Selena grew up in Texas, she could buy pickles in movie theaters! But pickles are just the beginning of Selena's odd snacking habits. She also loves to eat lemons sprinkled with salt! "It actually started when I did *Barney*. At lunch, my friend Demi and a bunch of other castmates would put sugar on their lemons, but I didn't like it. It was too sweet. So I put salt on it, and I fell in love with it ever since," Selena told *Girls' Life* magazine.

Of course a good snack wouldn't be complete without a yummy drink. Selena's favorite is "sugar-free Red Bull! I had a sip of my mom's and I was like, 'Oooh, this is good!' but she won't let me have too many. But every now and then, if I have a meeting or something, she'll let me. It gives me a little jolt of energy so I can focus on work or something!" Selena explained to *Popstar!*

Selena is confident, successful, and has every right to be proud of her many accomplishments. She has a wonderful supportive family and many fun, creative friends she enjoys spending time with. So whether she is goofing around watching movies, skateboarding, or surfing, Selena will always make the most of her time with her good friends and loving family!

CHAPTER 10:
Giving Back

Giving back to her community and using her popularity to increase awareness for causes that are important to her are high on Selena's list of priorities. "I'm very happy that I have a voice, and I'm going to use it," Selena told *Scholastic News* about her involvement in charities and other public service organizations. Selena knows she has been blessed with a successful career, a loving family, and a safe home, but she also knows that not everyone is as lucky as she is. So she always makes time in her busy schedule to contribute her money, time, and voice to causes that are important to her.

Selena works with several charities, including UNICEF and the AmberWatch Foundation. AmberWatch is an organization that helps educate kids and their parents about keeping kids safe from predators. Selena wants to make sure every child knows how to stay safe in every situation. She also works with other young volunteers at events and brainstorms new ideas to help prevent child abductions.

In the fall of 2008, Selena was named the youngest ever spokesperson for the Trick-or-Treat for UNICEF campaign. She told *Seventeen* magazine how excited she was about the honor. "I was recently competing for UNICEF's [2008 Trick-or-Treat campaign] spokesperson, and I freaked out when I got that!" It was the 58th anniversary of the United Nations Children's Fund event. The Trick-or-Treat campaign encourages children in America to make Halloween really count by collecting money instead of candy to benefit other children around the world. Selena even travelled to Ghana to help promote UNICEF and work with the volunteers there. It was a life-changing experience for Selena and she is dedicated to encouraging her fans to get involved, too!

A month later, during the 2008 presidential election, Selena became involved with UR Votes Count, a nationwide campaign devoted to educating teens on the importance of voting. She feels it is important for kids to understand the political process. All of the issues raised around a big election can get confusing — especially since both candidates sincerely believe that they can help the country the most. UR Votes Count helps kids understand the issues and clarifies exactly where each side stands objectively. Selena definitely wants teens to stay informed about politics after the election to make sure they still have a voice.

In spring of 2009, Selena lent her voice to a new cause that she felt was in line with her overall goal of helping kids and teens stay safe. Selena filmed two public service announcements for State Farm aimed at helping young drivers stay safe behind the wheel and reduce the number of fatal car crashes every year. These spots aired on the Disney Channel. Selena is a very safe and responsible driver and hopefully her encouragement is inspiring other teens to be safe, too!

In addition to teen safety, one of Selena's most important interests is the environment. Biology has always been Selena's favorite subject, as she explained to *Girls' Life* magazine: "I have no idea why, but there's something about learning about our planet and everything else, even the specific things like learning about flowers or something. I really love it." Lately, Selena has been learning a lot about the dangers that pollution and global warming pose, and it has really inspired her to get involved.

Protecting the ocean and beaches is especially important to Selena since she loves surfing so much!

Even when Selena doesn't have time in her busy

schedule to do big things to help the environment, she makes sure she does the little things that help every day. "We just want to do as much as possible. We recycle; we do everyday little things that people don't think will matter. But in reality, those little things are the most important. Doing everything you can and spreading the word," she told *Girl's Life* magazine. Selena would want her fans to do those little things, too — like recycling, using less water, and turning off the lights when you leave a room! While Selena was in Puerto Rico filming the *Wizards of Waverly Place* movie, she decided to join DoSomething.org and helped feed stray puppies! Selena has four dogs herself, so saving animals from neglect and abuse will always be an important cause for her!

Selena is asked to make a lot of public appearances, too. She presents awards, attends premieres and concerts, and goes to media events promoting worthy organizations. Selena is happy to attend, especially when the event is for a good cause! Selena's life is a whirlwind of work and activities these days, but she has always been willing to take the time to support her favorite charities and to use her star power to stand up for what she believes in. She hopes that her willingness to get involved and take a stand will inspire her fans to get involved, too!

CHAPTER 11:
Stylin' with Selena

Selena's look has really evolved since the first season of *Wizards of Waverly Place*. She used to live in skinny pants, graphic T-shirts, chunky jewelry, vests, bright colors, and, of course, Converse! Selena told PBSKids.org, "I'm a huge Converse girl. I think I have about twenty pairs in different colors." But these days, you are more likely to see Selena sporting sweet feminine dresses from top designers, sophisticated tops and jeans, and awesome high heels.

As she's matured, Selena has developed a serious interest in fashion and loves experimenting with different looks. Selena told *OK!* magazine, "I used to be 'a tomboy,' but over the past year my wardrobe's gotten classier. I'm growing up." Selena knows her look will change and evolve over time, and she believes that the important thing isn't what she wears, it's the way that she wears it. "Self-confidence is a huge part of it. You can't think that you're not as good as anyone else. And I think it's important to be careful of what you do and say and who you hang out with. Represent yourself well, even in the clothes you wear," Selena explained to PBSKids.org.

Selena has great style, so it's no wonder that fans love to copy her look. "I'm usually so casual. But little girls have come up to me, and they show me that they dress like me. A girl brought me a picture and said, 'I dressed up like you for school,' and it almost made me cry," she told *Girls' Life* magazine.

Imitation is definitely okay with Selena — she's even developed her own clothing line for K-Mart called Dream Out Loud. Selena worked with designers to pull the line together, but she was very involved, approving every single detail! She wanted to make sure there were pieces that would appeal to lots of different types of girls and it definitely shows. There are flirty skirts and dresses, cute skinny pants, and flowy tops that any girl can wear and feel pretty in! Selena wears a lot of the pieces herself and loves seeing her designs on fans! Of course, no matter what you are wearing, the easiest way to nab Selena's style is to copy her confidence. As long as you feel great in what you're wearing, you will look just as fab as she always does!

CHAPTER 12:
What's Next?

Selena is a star with a very bright future indeed. She has already established herself as an incredible actress, dancer, and singer — and there is tons more to come! *Wizards of Waverly Place* may be over, but that certainly doesn't mean Selena will be giving up on acting! She is very focused on expanding her acting skills with more film roles. Selena is being very picky about which roles she accepts because she does not want to get locked into a specific stereotype. She can do comedy, drama, and even voiceover work without breaking a sweat, so her future possibilities are really limitless!

As much as Selena loves acting, she would like to try her hand at other parts of the entertainment industry, too. Selena's mom Mandy's production company, July Moon Productions, is looking for great feature films to produce that Selena can star in. "I'll have my own control of my career and what my movie decisions will be," Selena told *E! Online.* "I want to make sure I choose roles that will challenge me as an actress." Selena is very excited about the possibility of producing a film as well as starring in it. She's had a lot of experience over the past few years and is hoping to bring some fresh, new ideas to her work behind the camera.

Music will always be a big part of Selena's life as well. She's experimented with different styles of music on each of her three albums and loves trying new things with her band. Fans should definitely expect that to continue! Touring is very important to Selena as well. She loves traveling to new cities and getting to meet and connect with her fans in person. Her tours have gotten larger and larger, and it won't be too long before she's selling out an arena near you!

No matter what the future holds for Selena, you can be sure that she will remain the same, sweet Texas girl she's always been. Her star continues to burn brighter and brighter and Hollywood will never be the same!

CHAPTER 13:
Just the Facts

FULL NAME: Selena Marie Gomez

NICKNAME: Sel

BIRTH DATE: July 22, 1992

HOMETOWN: Grand Prairie, Texas

HEIGHT: 5' 5"

HAIR COLOR: Dark brown

EYE COLOR: Brown

PARENTS: Mom: Mandy Teefy; stepdad: Brian
Teefy; dad: Ricardo Gomez

SIBLINGS: None

FAVORITE THANKSGIVING FOOD: Stuffing

FAVORITE PIZZA TOPPINGS: Cheese, mushrooms, jalapeño peppers

FAVORITE SNACKS: Dill pickles, lemons with salt

FAVORITE FRUIT: Mangos

FAVORITE SUBJECT: Biology

FAVORITE GADGET: iPhone

FAVORITE MOVIE: *The Wizard of Oz*

FAVORITE ACTRESS: Rachel McAdams

HOBBIES: Painting and drawing, singing, surfing, skateboarding, playing basketball

PETS: Four dogs

CHAPTER 14:
Selena Online

Want more Selena? Here is a list of extremely cool and interesting websites that have tons of information on Selena Gomez. If you want to find out what she's been doing, saying, or wearing, these are the sites to visit!

You can do a lot of cool stuff on the Internet, like play games, chat with friends, or even watch your favorite episodes of *Wizards of Waverly Place*. But Selena would always want you to be careful when you are hanging out online. Always get your parents permission to surf the web. And never try to meet someone in person that you met online or give out any sort of personal information, like your name, address, phone number, or the name of your school or sports team.

www.selenagomez.com

This is Selena's official website that has it all — the latest music, photos, and messages from Selena to her fans, and some of her YouTube videos along with links to her other official sites.

www.myspace.com/selenagomez

This is Selena's official MySpace page with her updated blog.

www.tv.disney.go.com/disneychannel/wizardsof waverlyplace/index.html

This is the official *Wizards of Waverly Place* Disney Channel site and it has tons of fun videos, activities, and information about Selena and the rest of the cast.

CHAPTER 15:
Quiztastic!

Would you and Selena be BFFs?

You are a big Selena fan, but would she and you hit it off? Take the quiz below to find out if you and Selena have what it takes to be best buds!

1. At the beach you can be found:

    a. making a sandcastle and flirting with cute boys

    b. lounging in the sun with a good book

    c. surfing

2. You are throwing a big party for your birthday. What's the most important thing for you?

a. that there is a big dance floor and rockin' music

b. that all of your different groups of friends get along and have fun

c. that there are plenty of snacks!

3. **Your best friend just got dumped. To cheer her up you:**

    a. crack jokes about her ex to make her laugh

    b. make her Rice Krispies and let her cry it out

    c. challenge her to a basketball game to help her get her anger out on the court

4. **For a Saturday night with friends you plan**

    a. a trip to the local karaoke lounge to belt out all your favorite songs

    b. a movie night with lots of yummy snacks

    c. a trip to the skate park to show off your moves and hang out

5. For the school dance you wear:

    a. a brightly colored, girly dress that really stands out

    b. a simple dress with shoes you can dance in

    c. a skirt and top with brightly colored Converse sneakers

Now count up your answers to see if you and Sel could be friends forever!

If you chose mostly A's, then you love the spotlight — just like Selena. You are funny and talented. Selena loves to laugh and has a real flair for comedy so you two would make an unstoppable duo. You would have a blast cracking each other up! Plus, you'd always be the life of every party with your silly antics.

If you chose mostly B's, then you and Selena would totally bond over your laid-back ways. You both hate drama, so you like to keep things simple. You are always honest with your friends and are there to support them, but you don't get overly involved in their problems. You would be the go-to pair for advice and hanging out!

If you chose mostly C's then you and sporty Selena would totally get along. You both love playing sports — especially basketball, surfing, and skateboarding. But you have a girly side, too, and so does Selena. So you would have a lot of fun together hanging with your guy friends *and* going out shopping together!

Now that you've taken this super fun quiz, share it with your friends. Chances are they are Selena fans who will love it just as much as you!